Poetry of the
Second World War

POETRY
OF THE SECOND
WORLD WAR

Selected by
EDWARD HUDSON

Dedicated to my mother's two brothers

Second Lieutenant Edward Kempthorne of the 25th Battalion,
New Zealand Infantry. Killed in action at Ruweisat Ridge,
south of El Alamein on 9 August 1942
and
Surgeon–Commander Humphrey de Bohun Kempthorne R.N.,
lost at sea on H.M.S. *Charybdis* on 23 October 1943

Designer: David Armitage
Editor: Susannah Foreman

First published in 1990 by
Wayland (Publishers) Ltd,
61 Western Road, Hove,
East Sussex BN3 1JD

Typeset, printed and bound by Butler & Tanner Ltd, Frome and London

British Library Cataloguing in Publication Data
Poetry of the Second World War. – (poetry of the World Wars).
  I. Title   II. series   1. Poetry in English, 1900–1945 – Anthologies
  821.912

ISBN 1–85210–959–9

CONTENTS

Preface

Edward Hudson's aptly chosen and skilfully arranged anthology is a worthy successor to his first work, *Poetry of the First World War*. In both volumes something is revealed of the inner thoughts and feelings of those whose lives were overtaken, suddenly and furiously, by war. Between the two anthologies I find a significant difference in style, a mirror of the difference in the scale and nature of the two wars themselves.

In the first it is the sheer horror of life in the trenches that predominates, leaving one almost speechless. Even after having experienced a major war myself, I still do not understand how men could endure what they did and keep on going. By contrast the Second World War was a far more complex, wide-ranging affair. In it, as Churchill said, 'The whole of the warring nations are involved, not only soldiers but the entire population, men, women and children ... The front lines run through the factories. The workmen are soldiers with different weapons but the same courage.' It was a war that inflicted as much anguish on the civilians as it did on the fighting man, indeed in some cases perhaps even more. Where, for instance, in the whole of recorded history is there evidence of suffering equal in volume and intensity to that of the Nazi concentration camps? What of the non-combatants who endured the year-long siege of Leningrad, or those who were exposed to the more ferocious elements of the bomber offensives?

These poems reflect the quantum leap that world war had now taken. Throughout the volume, but especially in the opening and closing sections, one feels a sense of outrage that mankind has been brought to such inhumane extremity. Here we find ourselves at the heart of the paradox of war, expressed by poets of many lands writing under widely differing circumstance – that even whilst one is driven to fight for what one believes to be a just cause, there is a side of one that shrinks from taking another person's life.

Leonard Cheshire

WAR POET

I am the man who looked for peace and found
My own eyes barbed.
I am the man who groped for words and found
An arrow in my hand.
I am the builder whose firm walls surround
A slipping land.
When I grow sick or mad
Mock me not nor chain me;
When I reach for the wind
Cast me not down
Though my face is a burnt book
And a wasted town.

Sidney Keyes

THE HOME FRONT

ACHTUNG! ACHTUNG!   **Mary Hacker**

I'm war. Remember me?
'Yes, you're asleep,' you say, 'and you kill men,'
Look in my game-bag, fuller than you think.

I kill marriages.
If one dies, one weeps and then heals clean.
(No scar without infection.) That's no good.
I can do better when I really try.
I wear down the good small faiths, enough
For little strains of peace, the near, the known,
But not for the big absence, man-sized silences,
Family pack of dangers, primate lusts
I hang on them.

I kill families.
Cut off the roots, the plant will root no more.
Tossed from thin kindness to thin kindness on
The child grows no more love; will only seek
A pinchbeck eros and a tawdry shock.
I teach the race to dread its unborn freak.
I maim well.

I drink gold.
How kind of you to pour it without stint
Into my sleeping throat. In case I die?
You think I'm god, the one that pours the most
Getting my sanction? Well, perhaps you're right.
Divert it, anyway, from the use of peace;
Keep the gross gaol, starvation and the lout,
The succulent tumour, loving bacillus, the clot
As bright as mine, friends all. I pop their prey
Into my bag.

I am the game that nobody can win.
What's yours is mine, what's mine is still my own.
I'm War. Remember me.

From *AUTUMN JOURNAL*   **Louis MacNeice**

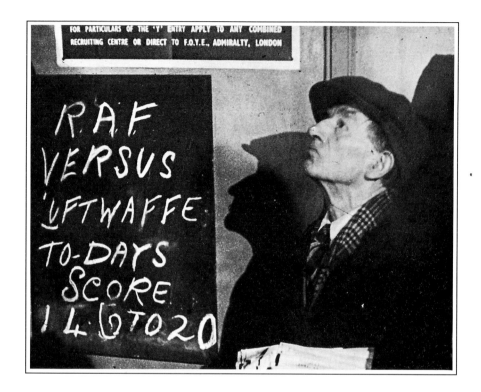

Today was a beautiful day, the sky was a brilliant
Blue for the first time for weeks and weeks
But posters flapping on the railings tell the fluttered
World that Hitler speaks, that Hitler speaks
And we cannot take it in and we go to our daily
Jobs to the dull refrain of the caption 'War'
Buzzing around us as from hidden insects
And we think 'This must be wrong, it has happened before,
Just like this before, we must be dreaming;
It was long ago these flies
Buzzed like this, so why are they still bombarding
The ears if not the eyes?'

And we laugh it off and go round town in the evening
And this, we say, is on me;
Something out of the usual, a Pimm's Number One, a Picon –
But did you see
The latest? You mean whether Cobb has just bust the record
Or do you mean the Australians have lost their last by ten
Wickets or do you mean that the autumn fashions –
No, we don't mean anything like that again.
No, what we mean is Hodza, Henlein, Hitler,
The Maginot Line,
The heavy panic that cramps the lungs and presses
The collar down the spine.
And when we go out into Piccadilly Circus
They are selling and buying the late
Special editions snatched and read abruptly
Beneath the electric signs as crude as Fate.
And the individual, powerless, has to exert the
Powers of will and choice
And choose between enormous evils, either
Of which depends on somebody else's voice.
The cylinders are racing in the presses,
The mines are laid,
The ribbon plumbs the fallen fathoms of Wall Street,
And you and I are afraid.

SHELLS

Wilfrid Gibson

All day like an automaton
She fits the shells into the gauge,
Hour after hour, to earn the wage
To keep her and her little son:
All day, hour after hour, she stands
Handling cold death with calloused hands.

She dare not think, she dare not feel
What happens to the shells that she
Handles and checks so carefully,
Or what, within each case of steel
Is packed as, hour by hour she stands
Handling cold death with calloused hands.

STATE OF READINESS H. B. Mallalieu

The moon rises late:
After sudden warning we wait,
The guns manned, searching among the stars.
At last, perhaps, our hour has come. Cars
Shoot past with urgent messages. We stand
Eager and glad, rifles steady and cool in hand.
For months nothing has happened. Now the sky
Turns hostile. Around us searchlights pry
Into thin clouds. Tonight the enemy, unseen,
Is real. We know these tedious past days have been
Prelude to battle: and if the time is near,
No dearer thoughts shall resurrect our fear.
For this we have waited. If the air should fill
With mushroom parachutes we will
Forsake all memory, all promises to break
On future days, for battle's compelling sake.

We have been ready. Though the warning prove
As false as any, we have abjured our love,
All dreams or hopes, to keep alert and sure.
The drone of planes continues and clouds endure
The searchlight's naked steel. Flares fall,
Hang in the sky. Flashes of guns appal
The quiet air. But as the minutes pass
Talk dies out, rats scurry through the grass.
We grow tired, long for cigarettes. Our minds return
To windows where familiar lights still burn.
Our thoughts resume their island voyages:
Raiders give place to homelier images.
The moon is full and shines
On tree and hill. In the farm a dog whines;
The routine of life continues while we wait;
Less eager and less certain. Our moons rise late.

POINT OF VIEW   **R. P. Brett**

(Heard in a butcher's shop, Bolton, Lancs.)

'It's slaughter – nothing more nor less –
The bombing in this war . . .
A dreadful thing . . . you'd never guess
The shocking sights we saw
In London, when the Blitz was on . . .
A leg hung from a tree;
A body with the top half gone
And nowt below the knee;
A hand with wedding ring and all;
Two feet in socks and boots;
A baby's head stuck to a shawl;
An arm torn by the roots;
While here and there was flesh in lumps
They shovelled into sacks.
It proper left us in the dumps . . .
Sent shivers down our backs.'

'It's slaughter, sir. I've seen a bit
Of what those swine can do.'
His chopper fell and fiercely split
A sheep's head clean in two.
'It's downright murder to attack
Defenceless folk who can't fight back!'
. . . And swinging dumbly on a hook,
A dead pig gave him such a look.

EVACUEE **Edith Pickthall**

The slum had been his home since he was born;
And then war came, and he was rudely torn
From all he'd ever known; and with his case
Of mean necessities, brought to a place
Of silences and space; just boom of sea
And sough of wind; small wonder then that he
Crept out one night to seek his sordid slum,
And thought to find his way. By dawn he'd come
A few short miles; and cattle in their herds
Gazed limpidly as he trudged by, and birds
Just stirring in first light, awoke to hear
His lonely sobbing, born of abject fear
Of sea and hills and sky; of silent night
Unbroken by the sound of shout and fight.

I remember waking
from a sort of sleep,
khaki–clad and rigid on the canvas bed,
gas mask already slung
like an obscene shoulder-bag;
torch in one hand, tin hat in the other,
and the blasted buzzer shaking
the waking brain to jelly,
mercilessly dragging the tired body up
out of exhausted oblivion.

First out tonight.
Feet into rubber boots,
stumble down the darkened corridor,
burst through the black-out into the noisy yard
where the cars stand patiently,
their burden of stretchers
outlined against a blazing sky.

Fumble for the lock of the old Ford –
'Put out that bloody torch!'
squeeze in behind the wheel, wait for the men;
three bearers pile in the back
loud with their cockney curses,
the leader beside me
'Now lads, remember there's a lidy in the car'.

Pull the starter, oh God make her go!
She goes. Across the yard,
double declutch at the gate, and out –
roaring down the now invisible road,
masked sidelights only –
roaring down to disaster;
where the bomb-ploughed houses wait
with their harvest of casualties.

His chair at the table, empty,
His home clothes hanging in rows forlorn
His cricket bat and cap, his riding cane.
The new flannel suit he had not worn
His dogs, restless, with tortured ears
Listening for his swift, light tread upon the path.
And there – his violin! Oh his violin! Hush! hold your tears.

For N. J. de B.-L. Crete, May 1941

YOUNG LADY DANCING
WITH SOLDIER

Phyllis Shand Allfrey

Young lady dancing with soldier,
Feeling stern peaty cloth with your slight hand,
So very happy,
So happy
To be dancing with the patriotic male –
You have forgotten
deliberately
(Or perhaps you were never concerned to know)
Last month your partner was a shipping clerk.

How, as he sat by his few inches of window,
This boy dreamed of ships and far engagements,
Battles with purpose
and future,
Fair women without guile, and England's honour,
Comme chevalier
sans peur . . .
But instead he got conscripted into the Army,
And now you are the last symbol of his dream.

It is rather thrilling to be a last symbol,
Before mud clogs the ears, blood frets the mouth
Of the poor clerk
turned soldier,
Whose highest fortune will be to find himself
Conscripted back
to life ...
Done up like a battered brown paper parcel –
No gentleman, *malgré tout*; clerk unemployed.

WAR BABY   **Pamela Holmes**

He has not even seen you, he
Who gave you your mortality;
And you, so small, how can you guess
His courage or his loveliness?

Yet in my quiet mind I pray
He passed you on the darkling way –
His death, your birth, so much the same –
And holding you, breathed once your name.

THESE ARE FACTS   Ruthven Todd

These are facts, observe them how you will:
Forget for a moment the medals and the glory,
The clean shape of the bomb, designed to kill,
And the proud headlines of the papers' story.

Remember the walls of brick that forty years
Had nursed to make a neat though shabby home;
The impertinence of death, ignoring tears,
That smashed the house and left untouched the Dome.

Bodies in death are not magnificent or stately,
Bones are not elegant that blast has shattered;
This sorry, stained and crumpled rag was lately
A man whose life was made of little things that mattered;

Now he is just a nuisance, liable to stink,
A breeding-ground for flies, a test-tube for disease:
Bury him quickly and never pause to think,
What is the future worth to men like these?

People are more than places, more than pride;
A million photographs record the works of Wren;
A city remains a city on credit from the tide
That flows among its rocks, a sea of men.

COCKEREL COMPLEX

R. P. Brett

The cockerel stands awhile, alert,
A creamy statue, ill at ease;
His left claw lifted from the dirt
Of scrabbled grass beneath the trees.

Across his arching back, the sheen
Of pearly plumage meets a veil
Of sulky shot-silk black and green
That flickers in his ruffling tail.

Suspicion lulled, his pendant claw
Descends to earth; he struts away
To rustle in the scattered straw
Around the golden chunks of hay.

The bloody ratchet of his comb
Saws back and forward in his stride;
His beady eye surveys his home,
His servile, questing hens, with pride.

He halts ... and from a stabbing beak
Resounds the raucous, screeching call ...
Continued by a mocking shriek
In echo from the farmhouse wall.

The quaking orchard hears him out –
For can the arrogance far-hurled
Mean anything but 'Who dares doubt
That I am king of this – my world?'

The farmer straightens from his toil
And, shielding eyes with sweating hand,
While gazing at the greening soil,
Exults, 'I'm master of my land!'

Before the clustered microphones,
Dictators mouth their sophistry;
Fanatical, or staid their tones,
They gloat, 'My Nation!', inwardly.

While God, in spite of godless war ...
The doubts to which swift death gives birth,
Is none the less proprietor
And partial to a proud 'My Earth!'

And in the great Infinity,
Beyond the tracks that planets plod,
A far superior Deity
Satirically sighs, 'My God!'

AT SEA

DESTROYERS IN THE ARCTIC　　　**Alan Ross**

Camouflaged, they detach lengths of sea and sky
When they move; offset, speed and direction are a lie.

Everything is grey anyway; ships, water, snow, faces.
Flanking the convoy, we rarely go through our paces:

But sometimes on tightening waves at night they wheel
Drawing white moons on strings from dripping keel.

Cold cases them, like ships in glass; they are formal,
Not real, except in adversity. Then, too, have to seem normal.

At dusk they intensify dusk, strung out, non-committal:
Waves spill from our wake, crêpe paper magnetised by gun metal.

They breathe silence, less solid than ghosts, ruminative
As the Arctic breaks up on their sides and they sieve

Moisture into mess-decks. Heat is cold-lined there,
Where we wait for a torpedo and lack air.

Repetitive of each other, imitating the sea's lift and fall,
On the wings of the convoy they indicate rehearsal.

Merchantmen move sideways, with the gait of crustaceans,
Round whom like eels escorts take up their stations.

Landfall, Murmansk; but starboard now a lead-coloured
Island, Jan Mayen. Days identical, hoisted like sails, blurred.

Counters moved on an Admiralty map, snow like confetti
Covers the real us. We dream we are counterfeits tied to our jetty.

But cannot dream long; the sea curdles and sprawls,
Liverishly real, and merciless all else away from us falls.

With the ship burning in their eyes
The white faces float like refuse
In the darkness – the water screwing
Oily circles where the hot steel lies.

They clutch with fingers frozen into claws
The lifebelts thrown from a destroyer,
And see, between the future's doors,
The gasping entrance of the sea.

Taken on board as many as lived, who
Had a mind left for living and the ocean,
They open eyes running with surf,
Heavy with the grey ghosts of explosion.

The meaning is not yet clear,
Where daybreak died in the smile –
And the mouth remained stiff
And grinning, stupid for a while.

But soon they joke, easy and warm,
As men will who have died once
Yet somehow were able to find their way –
Muttering this was not included in their pay.

Later, sleepless at night, the brain spinning
With cracked images, they won't forget
The confusion and the oily dead,
Nor yet the casual knack of living.

TO A GERMAN AIRMAN

Brian Gallie

Who flew slowly through the British Fleet

Perhaps you knew not what you did,
That what you did was good;
Perhaps the head I saw was dead,
Or blind with its own blood.

Perhaps the wings you thought you ruled,
With sky and sea beneath,
Beat once with love for God above –
And flew you to your death.

Perhaps: but I prefer to think
That something in you, friend,
No inch would give to land and live,
But conscious chose the end.

That something in you, like a bird,
Knowing no cage's bars,
Courage supreme – an instant dream
Of mind beneath the stars:

Misguided, arrogant, or proud,
But – beyond telling – great,
Made you defy our fire and fly
Straight on, to meet your fate.

Steel-capped, we cowered as you went,
Defiant and alone;
A noble thing, we watched you wing
Your way to the unknown.

You passed us, still a mile from death,
Rocked by the wind of shell;
We held our breath, until to death
Magnificent you fell.

Whatever comet lit your track –
Contempt, belief, or hate –
You let us see an enemy
Deliberately great.

WAR'S BENEFIT

Brian Gallie

We had not heard the music in men's laughter
Until we heard them crying as they died.
All their proud beauty, glory of glance and mien –
We only saw these after,
When they slid overside
At dusk, into the rushing of the wake.
Silence and Peace were words until we'd been
Shipmates with noise and danger, and could take
No respite. Were there colours to the sea?
Did beauty dance or dream
In ever-new perspective, shade and shape
Of cloud? And did it seem,
Before, that there could be
A measure of the distance to a star
Within the brain that wandered –
Behind the eye
Seeking in sea and sky
For death – and found escape
In gardens of strange beauty, where it pondered
On this strange gift of War?
This bounteous giving
To sense and ear and eye ...
Our youth took fire, and flamed with the wonderful living
We only learned when we were asked to die.
So, for the spell allowed us, we have laughed
The louder for the crying;
Thrown back our heads and quaffed
A sparkling magic, gulping, naked-throated,
Divine, insidious wine. There's no denying
The taste once learned; for to be so elated
Is worth all danger – even what we'll find
If the Gods show they love us, and are kind.

After the attack
In the warm blue seas
We lazed and lolled
Floating at ease
As the long waves rolled
But men in the morning
Bomb blasted sea choked
Floundered and gasped
In these same blue seas
Some dead some drowned
Some rescued maybe
But we the killers
Lazed and lolled
Floating at ease
As the long waves rolled

CORVETTE

Dully she shudders at the solid water,
A pause, and spray stings angrily over.
She plunges, and the noisy foam leaps widely
Marbling the moon-grey sea. Loud in the shrouds
Untrammelled winds roar songs of liberty.
Free as the petrels hovering astern
Her long lithe body answers to the swell.

Pardon if all the cleanness and the beauty
Brave rhythm and the immemorial sea
Ensnare us sometimes with their siren song,
Forgetful of our murderous intentions.
Through our uneasy peacetime carnival
Cold sweat of death rained on us like a dew;
Even this grey machinery of murder
Holds beauty and the promise of a future.

WHEN THE PLANE DIVED — **Wilfrid Gibson**

When the plane dived and the machine-gun spattered
The deck, in his numb clutch the tugging wheel
Bucked madly as he strove to keep the keel
Zig-zagging through the steep and choppy sea –
To keep zig-zagging, that was all that mattered ...
To keep the ship zig-zagging endlessly,
Dodging that diving devil. Now again
The bullets spattered like a squall of rain
About him; and again with desperate grip
He tugged, to port the helm ... to keep the ship
Zig-zagging ... zig-zagging through eternity;
To keep the ship ... A sudden scalding pain
Shot through his shoulder and the whole sky shattered
About him in red fire; and yet his grip
Tightened upon the wheel ... To keep the ship ...
Zig ... zig ... zig-zagging, that was all that mattered.

FOREIGN COMMISSION   **Norman Hampson**

November's anger flays all northern seas
And whips great weals across the slaty waste,
The sheering bows fling wide the broken water
It tumbles off the focsles, bitter spray
Knifes by the lively bridges bursting through
And low hulls welter in the marbled water.

On cabin panelling the pictures hold
Their balance in a world swung all awry,
On the damp mess decks now the lisping water
Slides with the restless hours, the cable bangs
Its slow mad rhythm in the naval pipes
And close-packed hammocks jostle all the night.

From heaving tables spins the inky thread
Leading from Theseus through the maze of time
To inland homes where seas are images;
These faded photographs hold frozen truth,
Quick smile, blown hair, in lines map-accurate,
The contour skeleton of living land.

Through all the shapeless months these minds support
Fading perspectives with their wishful dreams,
Assurance grows appeal, their letters scream,
Their own alarm makes fact of all their fear,
The woman's boredom stares between the lines;
And then the silence and the anxious faces.

These are your heroes, whom tomorrow's dawn
May find half-frozen in an oily sea;
They have their memories, their friends who were,
They know the shapes of death and dare forget,
But slow corrosion rusts their lives away
And etches grief on brows that should be young.

There are no killers here, whom crusted pride
Armours against their own humanity,
Or bigot's eyes can blind to bloody hands;
The quiet counties are their pedigree
Whose honest living asks no easy answer
Nor moves the goal to meet their straying ways.

Look for no tragic actors great in stature,
Whose blazing hearts might kindle half a world,
These lives obscure, only their sorrows vast
Winds of humanity that sigh by night
Through all the peopled earth; the men who bear
A fate acceptance cannot make less real.

WAR IN THE AIR

They told me, when they cut the ready wheat
the hares are suddenly homeless and afraid,
and aimlessly run the stubble with scared feet
finding no homes in sunlight or in shade.
– It's morning, and the Hampdens have returned,
the crews are home, have stretched and laughed and gone:
whence the planes came and the bright neon burned
the sun has ridden the sky and made the dawn.
He walks distraught, circling the landing ground,
waiting the last one in that won't come back,
and like those hares, he wanders round and round,
lost and desolate on the close-cropped track.

HIGH FLIGHT   **John Magee**

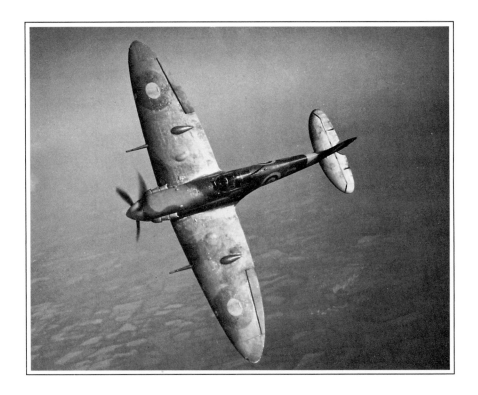

Oh! I have slipped the surly bonds of Earth
And danced the skies on laughter-silvered wings;
Sunward I've climbed, and joined the tumbling mirth
Of sun-split clouds – and done a hundred things
You have not dreamed of – wheeled and soared and swung
High in the sunlit silence. Hov'ring there,
I've chased the shouting wind along, and flung
My eager craft through footless halls of air.
Up, up the long, delirious, burning blue
I've topped the wind-swept heights with easy grace
Where never lark, or even eagle flew.
And while with silent, lifting mind I've trod
The high untrespassed sanctity of space,
Put out my hand and touched the face of God.

John Bayliss

With broken wing they limped across the sky
caught in late sunlight, with their gunner dead,
one engine gone, – the type was out-of-date, –
blood on the fuselage turning brown from red:

knew it was finished, looking at the sea
which shone back patterns in kaleidoscope
knew that their shadow would meet them by the way,
close and catch at them, drown their single hope:

sat in this tattered scarecrow of the sky
hearing it cough, the great plane catching
now the first dark clouds upon her wing-base, –
patching the great tear in evening mockery.

So two men waited, saw the third dead face,
and wondered when the wind would let them die.

THE FURY OF AERIAL BOMBARDMENT

Richard Eberhart

You would think the fury of aerial bombardment
Would rouse God to relent; the infinite spaces
Are still silent. He looks on shock-pried faces.
History, even, does not know what is meant.

You would feel that after so many centuries
God would give man to repent; yet he can kill
As Cain could, but with multitudinous will,
No farther advanced than in his ancient furies.

Was man made stupid to see his own stupidity?
Is God by definition indifference, beyond us all?
Is the eternal truth man's fighting soul
Wherein the Beast ravens in its own avidity?

Of Van Wettering I speak, and Averill,
Names on a list, whose faces I do not recall
But they are gone to early death, who late in school
Distinguished the belt feed lever from the belt holding pawl.

THE DEATH OF THE BALL TURRET GUNNER

Randall Jarrell

From my mother's sleep I fell into the State,
And I hunched in its belly till my wet fur froze.
Six miles from earth, loosed from its dream of life,
I woke to black flak and the nightmare fighters.
When I died they washed me out of the turret with a hose.

SHORT LEAVE   **O. C. Chave**

I have heard long enough the roar,
The shrill cacophony
By aero-engines thrown
Through helmet, earpiece, bone
Into the shrinking brain,
And would no more
Abuse my gift of sense
With this loud-ringing
Madness bringing
Quintessence of metalled pain.

So let me soothe my ear
With other music, hear
The wakening of birds,
Wind in the rushes and a stream that tries
To swamp its stepping-stones, the plop
Of curious trout that rise
To view their vision's rounded top.
Then will I listen
My senses fasten
When passion's heat is spent
To the cool-fingered words
Of after-love and be content.

FLEET FIGHTER

Olivia FitzRoy

'Good show!' he said, leaned his head back and laughed.
'They're wizard types!' he said, and held his beer
Steadily, looked at it and gulped it down
Out of its jam-jar, took a cigarette
And blew a neat smoke ring into the air.
'After this morning's prang I've got the twitch;
I thought I'd had it in that teased-out kite.'
His eyes were blue, and older than his face,
His single stripe had known a lonely war
But all his talk and movements showed his age.
His whole life was the air and his machine,
He had no thought but of the latest 'mod',
His jargon was of aircraft or of beer.
'And what will you do afterwards?' I said,
Then saw his puzzled face, and caught my breath.
There was no afterwards for him, but death.

SEARCHLIGHTS OVER BERLIN   T. R. Hodgson

Their silver scalpels probe the wound of night
seeking our doom, a death
to death. And now
no highflung phrase, no braggart
gesture of the hand or jaw
can still the double fear. Who fly
ten thousand feet above in the shrill dark
are linked with those who cower
under earth to hear, vague as sea
upon an island wind, the murmur
which is, for some
eternity, for some
an ending,
And he is rising mad who searches here
for meaning.

PLACTIC AIRMAN   **Wrenne Jarman**

His face is smooth as sculptured faces are,
His features fair enough to draw a girl's
Arch backward glance, his disciplined blond curls
Swept from a grafted brow without a scar.

But this young mottled face does not betray,
As other faces do, the moods behind –
If he has secrets, they are locked away:
He looks out at the world from a drawn blind
Screening the man he was. And who was he?
Only the grave eyes know, and do not tell....

Be gentle with him, World, who has forgone
His unique pattern, his identity:
Be tender, lest the frozen mask should melt
Abruptly, and surprise us with its scorn.

'Clearing Black Section
Patrol Bass Rock,'
Leaps heart; after shock
Action comes stumbling;
Snatch your helmet;
Then run smoothly, to the grumbling
Of a dozing Merlin heating
Supercharged air,
You are there
By 'Z'.

Down hard on the behind
The parachute; you are blind
With your oxygen snout
But click, click, click, click, you feel
And the harness is fixed.
Round the wing
And 'Out of the cockpit, you,'
Clamber the rung
And the wing as if a wasp had stung
You, hop and jump into the cockpit,
Split second to spike
The Sutton harness holes,
One, two, three, four,

Thrust with your
Hand to the throttle open . . .

'*Operations*' called and spoken.

PARACHUTE DESCENT **David Bourne**

Snap back the canopy,
Pull out the oxygen tube,
Flick the harness pin
And slap out into the air
Clear of the machine.

Did you ever dream when you were young
Of floating through the air, hung
Between the clouds and the gay
Be-blossomed land?
Did you ever stand and say,
'To sit and think and be alone
In the middle of the sky
Is my one most perfect wish'?

That was a fore-knowing;
You knew that some day
To satiate an inward crave
You must play with the wave
Of a cloud. And shout aloud
In the clean air,
The untouched-by-worldly-things-and-mean air,
With exhilarated living.

You knew that you must float
From the sun above the clouds
To the gloom beneath, from a world
Of rarefied splendour to one
Of cheapened dirt, close-knit
In its effort to encompass man
In death.

So you can stay in the clouds, boy,
You can let your soul go onwards,
You have no ties on earth,
You could never have accomplished
Anything. Your ideas and ideals
Were too high. So you can stay
In the sky, boy, and have no fear.

CONSCRIPTS

ALL DAY IT HAS RAINED   **Alun Lewis**

All day it has rained, and we on the edge of the moors
Have sprawled in our bell-tents, moody and dull as boors,
Groundsheets and blankets spread on the muddy ground
And from the first grey wakening we have found
No refuge from the skirmishing fine rain
And the wind that made the canvas heave and flap
And the taut wet guy-ropes ravel out and snap.
All day the rain has glided, wave and mist and dream,
Drenching the gorse and heather, a gossamer stream
Too light to stir the acorns that suddenly
Snatched from their cups by the wild south-westerly
Pattered against the tent and our upturned dreaming faces.

And we stretched out, unbuttoning our braces,
Smoking a Woodbine, darning dirty socks,
Reading the Sunday papers – I saw a fox
And mentioned it in the note I scribbled home; –
And we talked of girls and dropping bombs on Rome,
And thought of the quiet dead and the loud celebrities
Exhorting us to slaughter, and the herded refugees;

– Yet thought softly, morosely of them, and as indifferently
As of ourselves or those whom we
For years have loved, and will again
Tomorrow maybe love; but now it is the rain
Possesses us entirely, the twilight and the rain.

And I can remember nothing dearer or more to my heart
Than the children I watched in the woods on Saturday
Shaking down burning chestnuts for the schoolyard's merry play,
Or the shaggy patient dog who followed me
By Sheet and Steep and up the wooded scree
To the Shoulder o' Mutton where Edward Thomas brooded long
On death and beauty – till a bullet stopped his song.

STEEL CATHEDRALS   D. Van den Bogaerde

It seems to me, I spend my life in stations.
Going, coming, standing, waiting.
Paddington, Darlington, Shrewsbury, York.
I know them all most bitterly.
Dawn stations, with a steel light, and waxen figures.
Dust, stone, and clanking sounds, hiss of weary steam.
Night stations, shaded light, fading pools of colour.
Shadows and the shuffling of a million feet.

Khaki, blue, and bulky kitbags, rifles gleaming dull.
Metal sound of army boots, and smoker's coughs.
Titter of harlots in their silver foxes.
Cases, casks, and coffins, clanging of the trolleys.
Tea urns tarnished, and the greasy white of cups.
Dry buns, Woodbines, Picture Post and Penguins;
and the blaze of magazines.
Grinding sound of trains, and rattle of the platform gates.
Running feet and sudden shouts, clink of glasses from the buffet.
Smell of drains, tar, fish and chips and sweaty scent, honk of taxis;
and the gleam of cigarettes.
Iron pillars, cupolas of glass, girders messed by pigeons;
the lazy singing of a drunk.
Sailors going to Chatham, soldiers going to Crewe.
Aching bulk of kit and packs, tin hats swinging.
The station clock with staggering hands and callous face,
says twenty-five-to-nine.
A cigarette, a cup of tea, a bun,
and my train goes at ten.

SQUADDING

Jack Lindsay

The sergeant's roar, interpreted aright
by instinct of fear, dies bouncing on the asphalt.
The squad, grey–denimed in the distinct light
stand–easy, adjust a cap or finger a belt.

Shedding its shell, a crab must feel like this,
lost between two worlds, not so much scared as wary.
They consider the sergeant without prejudice
and accept the insulting candour of his stare.

Why is it then that with arms and legs loosened
out of a random rhythm they are forced to move
in a strange unison? Apart from the nuisance,
there is a buoyancy, even a kind of love.

Yet still, as the clue's emerging, they feel again
that pull of difference splitting each life into two.
More than the sergeant, each stands apart. The brain
is numbed with a semi-defiance. It isn't true.

It isn't true, each insists. It isn't happening.
This is not me. But it is. And you grin to find
the will re-welded, richer. You lose your cap,
feel foolish; and an urgency raps your mind –

tightened, look, in the buckle of belt and sling,
jestingly sealed in each momentous trifle,
stamped now, clamped in the bolt and the bayonet-ring,
fondled and final in the uplifted rifle.

NAMING OF PARTS

Today we have naming of parts. Yesterday,
We had daily cleaning. And tomorrow morning,
We shall have what to do after firing. But today,
Today we have naming of parts. Japonica
Glistens like coral in all of the neighbouring gardens,
And today we have naming of parts.

This is the lower sling swivel. And this
Is the upper sling swivel, whose use you will see,
When you are given your slings. And this is the piling swivel,
Which in your case you have not got. The branches
Hold in the gardens their silent, eloquent gestures,
Which in our case we have not got.

This is the safety-catch, which is always released
With an easy flick of the thumb. And please do not let me
See anyone using his finger. You can do it quite easy
If you have any strength in your thumb. The blossoms
Are fragile and motionless, never letting anyone see
Any of them using their finger.

And this you can see is the bolt. The purpose of this
Is to open the breech, as you see. We can slide it
Rapidly backwards and forwards: we call this
Easing the spring. And rapidly backwards and forwards
The early bees are assaulting and fumbling the flowers:
They call it easing the Spring.

They call it easing the Spring: it is perfectly easy
If you have any strength in your thumb: like the bolt,
And the breech, and the cocking-piece, and the point of balance,
Which in our case we have not got; and the almond-blossom
Silent in all of the gardens and the bees going backwards and forwards,
For today we have naming of parts.

INTO BATTLE

THE SENTRY   **Alun Lewis**

I have begun to die.
For now at last I know
That there is no escape
From Night. Not any dream
Nor breathless images of sleep
Touch my bat's-eyes. I hang
Leathery-arid from the hidden roof
Of Night, and sleeplessly
I watch within Sleep's province.
I have left
The lovely bodies of the boy and girl
Deep in each other's placid arms;
And I have left
The beautiful lanes of sleep
That barefoot lovers follow to this last
Cold shore of thought I guard.
I have begun to die
And the guns' implacable silence
Is my black interim, my youth and age,
In the flower of fury, the folded poppy,
Night.

THE BATTLE   **Louis Simpson**

Helmet and rifle, pack and overcoat
Marched through a forest. Somewhere up ahead
Guns thudded. Like the circle of a throat
The night on every side was turning red.

They halted and they dug. They sank like moles
Into the clammy earth between the trees.
And soon the sentries, standing in their holes,
Felt the first snow. Their feet began to freeze.

At dawn the first shell landed with a crack.
Then shells and bullets swept the icy woods.
This lasted many days. The snow was black.
The corpses stiffened in their scarlet hoods.

Most clearly of that battle I remember
The tiredness in eyes, how hands looked thin
Around a cigarette, and the bright ember
Would pulse with all the life there was within.

I READ ABOUT TANK BATTLES — Bertolt Brecht

Translated by John Willett

You Augsburg dyer's son, once gamely striving
To match my skill at marbles long ago
Where are you now among the grey tanks driving
In clouds of dust to lay sweet Flanders low?

That bomb of flesh, chopped down above Calais
Was that the weaver's son whom I once knew?
Son of our baker in my childhood days
Was bleeding Artois's cry provoked by you?

From DUNKIRK　　　　　　　　　　　　**B. G. Bonallack**

All through the night, and in the next day's light
The endless columns came. Here was Defeat.
The men marched doggedly, and kept their arms,
But sleep weighed on their backs so that they reeled
Staggering as they passed. Their force was spent.
Only, like old Horatius, each man saw
Far off his home, and seeing, plodded on.
At last they ceased. The sun shone down, and we
Were left to watch along a dusty road.

That night we blew our guns. We placed a shell
Fuse downwards in each muzzle. Then we put
Another in the breech, secured a wire
Fast to the firing lever, crouched, and pulled.
It sounded like a cry of agony,
The crash and clang of splitting, tempered steel.
Thus did our guns, our treasured colours, pass;
And we were left bewildered, weaponless,
And rose and marched, our faces to the sea.

We formed in line beside the water's edge.
The little waves made oddly home-like sounds,
Breaking in half-seen surf upon the strand.
The night was full of noise; the whistling thud
The shells made in the sand, and pattering stones;
The cries cut short, the shouts of units' names;
The crack of distant shots, and bren gun fire;
The sudden clattering crash of masonry.

Steadily, all the time, the marching tramp
Of feet passed by along the shell-torn road,
Under the growling thunder of the guns.
The major said 'The boats cannot get in,
'There is no depth of water. Follow me.'
And so we followed, wading in our ranks
Into the blackness of the sea. And there,
Lit by the burning oil across the swell,
We stood and waited for the unseen boats.

Oars in the darkness, rowlocks, shadowy shapes
Of boats that searched. We heard a seaman's hail.
Then we swam out, and struggled with our gear,
Clutching the looming gunwales. Strong hands pulled,
And we were in and heaving with the rest,
Until at last they turned. The dark oars dipped,
The laden craft crept slowly out to sea,
To where in silence lay the English ships.

DISEMBARKATION

H. H. Tilley

Stooping, stumbling, swearing, dull-eyed men
Slouch in long lines across the slippery deck
Emerging slowly from their smelly pen –
Look out there or you'll break your blasted neck! –
And shamble to a blocked companion-way
Where drovers wait to urge them up and on,
While others, from the top, hold them at bay
Until a thousand more have safely gone.
Herded from the ship, they fill the quay
And shuffle into patient, waiting rows,
Helmeted, equipped and blancoed, three by three,
A phalanx dark in which each white face shows:
Then turn and march away who slayed the Hun
To seek the butchers of the Rising Sun.

INFANTRYMAN

Colin McIntyre

When you have walked through a town, as an infantryman,
You'll never go through streets the same way again.

There is shoulder-ache from rifle-sling, and sore
butt-bruise, of bolt, on hip and thigh.

The walk comes somewhere between lope and slow hike,
a wary step, splay-footed, as drawers cellular
catch in the crotch, twist centrifugally around.

Our lot moved at slow deliberate plod, eyes down, look out.
Ted walked on the left, looks right; I took the right,
looked left. Well spaced out, bloody tired all the time.

Ted and I had a reputation, in Four Section, for hitting
the deck, together, quick as a flash, at the first shell.
Ted had a nose for crossroads ranged by guns.

Infantrymen grow fat in later years, from never walking.
Ted would have become quite gross. But Ted's dead.
Stepped on an AP mine in champagne country.
Cheers, Ted, you old sod, you.

The guns know what is what, but underneath
In fearful file
We go around burst boots and packs and teeth
That seem to smile.

The scene jags like a strip of celluloid,
A mortar fires,
Cinzano falls, Michelin is destroyed,
The man of tyres.

As darkness drifts like fog in from the sea
Somebody says
'We're digging in'. Look well, for this may be
The last of days.

Hot lightnings stitch the blind eye of the moon,
The thunder's blunt.
We sleep. Our dreams pass in a faint platoon
Toward the front.

Sleep well, for you are young. Each tree and bush
Drips with sweet dew,
And earlier than morning June's cool hush
Will waken you.

The riflemen will wake and hold their breath.
Though they may bleed
They will be proud awhile of something death
Still seems to need.

WALKING WOUNDED   **Vernon Scannell**

A mammoth morning moved grey flanks and groaned.
In the rusty hedges pale rags of mist hung;
The gruel of mud and leaves in the mauled lane
Smelled sweet, like blood. Birds had died or flown,
Their green and silent attics sprouting now
With branches of leafed steel, hiding round eyes
And ripe grenades ready to drop and burst.
In the ditch at the cross-roads the fallen rider lay
Hugging his dead machine and did not stir
At crunch of mortar, tantrum of a Bren
Answering a Spandau's manic jabber.
Then into sight the ambulance came,
Stumbling and churning past the broken farm,
The amputated sign-post and smashed trees,
Slow wagonloads of bandaged cries, square trucks
That rolled on ominous wheels, vehicles
Made mythopoeic by their mortal freight
And crimson crosses on the dirty white.

This grave procession passed, though, for a while,
The grinding of their engines could be heard,
A dark noise on the pallor of the morning,
Dark as dried blood; and then it faded, died.
The road was empty, but it seemed to wait –
Like a stage which knows the cast is in the wings –
Wait for a different traffic to appear.
The mist still hung in snags from dripping thorns;
Absent-minded guns still sighed and thumped.
And then they came, the walking wounded,
Straggling the road like convicts loosely chained,
Dragging at ankles exhaustion and despair.
Their heads were weighted down by last night's lead,
And eyes still drank the dark. They trailed the night
Along the morning road. Some limped on sticks;
Others wore rough dressings, splints and slings;
A few had turbanned heads, the dirty cloth
Brown-badged with blood. A humble brotherhood,
Not one was suffering from a lethal hurt,
They were not magnified by noble wounds,
There was no splendour in that company.
And yet, remembering after eighteen years,
In the heart's throat a sour sadness stirs;
Imagination pauses and returns
To see them walking still, but multiplied
In thousands now. And when heroic corpses
Turn slowly in their decorated sleep
And every ambulance has disappeared
The walking wounded still trudge down that lane,
And when recalled they must bear arms again.

'LOVE LETTERS OF THE DEAD' **Douglas Street**
A Commando Intelligence Briefing

'Go through the pockets of the enemy wounded,
Go through the pockets of the enemy dead –
There's a lot of good stuff to be found there –
That's of course if you've time', I said.
'Love letters are specially useful,
It's amazing what couples let slip –
Effects of our bombs for example,
The size and type of a ship.
These'll all give us bits of our jigsaw.
Any questions?' I asked as per rule-book;
A close-cropped sergeant from Glasgow,
With an obstinate jut to his jaw,
Got up, and at me he pointed;
Then very slowly he said:
'Do you think it right, well I don't,
For any bloody stranger to snitch
What's special and sacred and secret,
Love letters of the dead?'

WINTER BILLET   **Peter Huchel**

Translated by Michael Hamburger

I sit by the shed,
Oiling my rifle.

A foraging hen
With her foot imprints
Lightly on snow
A script as old as the world,
A sign as old as the world,
Lightly on snow
The tree of life.

I know the butcher
And his way of killing.
I know the axe.
I know the chopping-block.

Across the shed
You will flutter,
Stump with no head,
Yet still a bird
That presses a twitching wing
Down on the split wood.

I know the butcher.
I sit by the shed,
Oiling my rifle.

FIRST SNOW IN ALSACE   **Richard Wilbur**

The snow came down last night like moths
Burned on the moon; it fell till dawn,
Covered the town with simple cloths.

Absolute snow lies rumpled on
What shellbursts scattered and deranged,
Entangled railings, crevassed lawn.

As if it did not know they'd changed,
Snow smoothly clasps the roofs of homes
Fear-gutted, trustless and estranged.

The ration stacks are milky domes;
Across the ammunition pile
The snow has climbed in sparkling combs.

You think: beyond the town a mile
Or two, this snowfall fills the eyes
Of soldiers dead a little while.

Persons and persons in disguise,
Walking the new air white and fine,
Trade glances quick with shared surprise.

At children's windows, heaped, benign,
As always, winter shines the most,
And frost makes marvellous designs.

The night-guard coming from his post,
Ten first-snows back in thought, walks slow
And warms him with a boyish boast:

He was the first to see the snow.

THE EASTERN FRONT

MARCHING PAST   **Michael Guttenbrunner**

Translated by Michael Hamburger

The finest singing I have ever heard
came from the throats of Russian soldiers,
close to starvation – they could hardly stand.
'Sing. If you sing you shall have some grub!'
So they began to sing. I, marching past there,
long after that could hear it, dying song.

From TO THE GERMAN SOLDIERS   **Bertolt Brecht**
IN THE EAST

Translated by John Willett

Brothers, if I were with you –
Were one of you out there in the eastern snowfields
One of the thousands of you amid the iron chariots –
I would say as you say: Surely
There must be a road leading home.

But brothers, dear brothers
Under my steel helmet, under my skull
I would know what you know: There
Is no longer a road leading home.

On the map in a schoolboy's atlas
The road to Smolensk is no bigger
Than the Führer's little finger, but
In the snowfields it is further
Very far, too far.

The snow will not last for ever, just till springtime.
But men will not last for ever either. Springtime
Will be too long.

Brothers, if I were with you
Were trudging with you across the icy wastes
I would ask as you ask: Why
Have I come here, whence
There is no longer any road leading home?

And I shall never again see
The land from which I came
Not the Bavarian forests, nor the southern mountains
Not the sea, not the moors of Brandenburg, the pinetrees
Nor the Franconian vineyards sloping down to the river
Not in the grey dawn, not at midday
And not as evening falls.

Nor the cities and the city were I was born.
Nor will I or you
Hear the voice of wives and mothers
Or the wind in the chimney in our homes
Or the cheerful sounds of the city, or the bitter.

No, I shall die in the prime of my life
Unloved, unmissed
A war device's reckless driver.

Untaught, save in my last hour
Untried, save in murdering
Not missed, save by the slaughterers.

And I shall lie under the earth
Which I have ravaged
A vandal without friends.
A sigh of relief will go up over my grave.

For what will they be burying?
A hundredweight of meat in a tank, soon to rot.
What will come of it?
A shrivelled bush, all frozen
A mess they shovelled away
A smell blown away by the wind.

Brothers, if I were now with you
On the road back to Smolensk
Back from Smolensk to nowhere

I would feel what you feel: From the start
I knew under my steel helmet, under my skull
That bad is not good
That two and two make four
And that all will die who went with him
The bloodstained bawler
The bloodstained fool.

Who did not know that the road to Moscow is long
Very long, too long.
That the winter in Eastern Europe is cold
Very cold, too cold.
That the peasants and workers of the new state would
Defend their earth and their cities
Till we are all blotted out.

They heard no mother's sweet lullabying,
They did not listen to grandfather's tales,
Only harsh voices of tanks terrified them,
Alarmed by widows' heartrending wails.

They wept not through sleepless nights of the battle,
Carried safe down to the cellars from bed,
And the first words which they learned to prattle
Were about Nazi and fighting and bread.

The strife will grow quiet. The foeman be humbled.
The children all long for that day, one and all,
When from the clouds, like warm raindrops tumbling,
Down on war's ashes thick silence will fall.

They will venture from home to the fields, shyly doubtful,
So that, the first time in their lives, they in peace
Can delight in their own native landscape about them,
And hear the bell of a brook in the reeds.

The scent of the fields, the woods' beauty delight you,
But their hearts will still tremble from fear many days,
They will see in the first stork an aeroplane flying,
They will see in first dawn-light a city ablaze.

The thunder beyond the far woods gently booming
Will bring back the terror of bombing once more,
And often, yes often, through their pure dreams looming,
Loudly the voices of battle will roar.

THE PANES OF AN OLD MANSION

Maksim Tank

Translated by Vera Rich

Very carefully,
Wipe the window-panes clean
Of this old mansion!
There have survived such a few of them
Of all that were in my city.

They have seen far, far more than
The trees and the monuments.
They have seen far, far more than
The eyes of mere men
Which always grew dim when the shooting
Was over.

Very carefully,
Wipe the window-panes clean
Lest with shadows of smoke
From fires of war
You wipe off the shadows
Of those close to you
Who for the very last time
Once looked out through the panes of these windows.

THE HERO

Pimien Pancanka

Translated by Vera Rich

He angrily said 'Troops! Get up. Hustle!
This is no beach, this is war! Don't slack!'
And he lay on the snaked coils of wire. And, mustered,
Two hundred soldiers boots, worn and dusty
Passed on over his back.

Not he, but others attacked, were hurling
Grenades into concrete pillboxes there,
They ran through Fritzes, set tanks burning
And hoisted the victory flag in the morning
Over the conquered frontier.

But he, from the rusted barbs releasing,
Plucked his bones without groaning, with his own hand,
Collapsed in the grass, as a pain unceasing
To grasses, to dewdrops and soothing breezes
Which from the Valdai lakes gently fanned.

IDENTITY DISC

Maksim Tank

Translated by Vera Rich

This identity disc cast from a stainless alloy, Number
Seven million three hundred and forty-five,
I found in a field where foeman soldiers in inglorious slumber
Sleep, where the rye, blooming, rustling, thrives.

I wipe it clean of all the sand. And who were you, then, fallen foeman,
Your symbol to your kin I'd like to give,
But I do not know your name, your family and where is your hometown,
Seven million three hundred and forty-five!

I only know: your general, some Kriegswulf or von Spadel's aiming
With his imperialists that war should thrive.
Rise up, and lest the years prepare new death, call to your own by name,
   friend
Seven million three hundred and forty-five.

Surely you'll not allow your son, having lost his youth and honour,
To tread that one-way road so that they'll fix
Upon his breast another mark of death that bears the number on it:
Seven million three hundred and forty-six.

WAR IN THE DESERT

The net like a white vault, hung overhead
Dewy and glistening in the full moon's light,
Which cast a shadow-pattern of the thread
Over our face and arms, laid still and white
Like polished ivories on the dark bed.
The truck's low side concealed from us the sight
Of tents and bivouacs and track-torn sand
That lay without; only a distant sound
Of gunfire sometimes or, more close at hand,
A bomb, with dull concussion of the ground,
Pressed in upon our world, where, all else banned,
Our lonely souls eddied like echoing sound
Under the white cathedral of the net,
And like a skylark in captivity
Hung fluttering in the meshes of our fate,
With death at hand and, round, eternity.

MEDJEZ-EL-BAB

C. H. Bevan

Shell shattered tanks, seared hulls burned red with fire;
Steel helmets, broken rifles, coils of wire;
Beside the track, abandoned guns point blind at vanished targets;
Here's the cast down rind of yesterday's battle.
Only yesterday
This plain was loud with guns and all ablaze with our attack.
Now new men come to gaze
Uncomprehending.
How can we explain
the tension and the tumult and the pain
of yesterday?
Dulled voices ask
what came ye forth to seek?
Astonishment and drama here revealed?
There's nothing that's so rustily antique
as yesterday's battlefield.

From *PORTRAIT AND BACKGROUND*

James Walker

Tobruk way were the graves. Not many,
As numbers go, as casualties in war,
Though in the isolating moon they seemed
Milestones over the world, and in the sunlight
Their identities oppressed, as all things did
In that meticulous vivisecting light.
Most were anonymous, the scattered ones,
With stones heaped over them to keep their bones
Longer, a little, from jackals and the raven.
'*Ein unbekannter englischer Soldat*'
Held a wild place where there were flowers and larks.
But that was gracious. Most were '*Unbekannt*',
'*Incognito*', 'Unknown'. These haunted most.
For these were us. This was the end we came to,
Whether our bones went underground or not.
Love's individuality became
Ein unbekannter englischer Soldat.
So we despised our bodies, whose too-tired flesh
No longer brought us in its old delights.
And sometimes in the dark, running for shelter,
We stumbled over them, and cursed these dead
Equally with the living, lying still.

GALLANTRY   **Keith Douglas**

The colonel in a casual voice
spoke into the microphone a joke
which through a hundred earphones broke
into the ears of a doomed race.

Into the ears of the doomed boy, the fool
whose perfectly mannered flesh fell
in opening the door for a shell
as he had learnt to do at school.

Conrad luckily survived the winter:
he wrote a letter to welcome
the suspicious spring: only his silken
intentions severed with a single splinter.

Was George fond of little boys?
we always suspected it,
but who will say: since George was hit
we never mention our surmise.

It was a brave thing the colonel said,
but the whole sky turned too hot
and the three heroes never heard what
it was, gone deaf with steel and lead.

But the bullets cried with laughter,
the shells were overcome with mirth,
plunging their heads in steel and earth –
(the air commented in a whisper).

THE TAKING OF THE KOPPIE   Uys Krige

No, it was only a touch of dysentery, he said. He was doing fine now thank
    you ... What the hell were the chaps grousing about anyhow?
He was sitting on the edge of his hospital cot clad only in a slip with both
    his feet on the floor,
his strong young body straight and graceful as a tree, golden as any
    pomegranate but only firmer,
its smooth surface uncracked, gashed with no fissure by the burning blazing
    sun of war;
and with his muscles rippling lightly
like a vlei's shallows by the reeds touched by the first breath of the wind of
    dawn.
as he swung his one leg over on to the other.

He was telling us about the death of the colonel and the major whom all
    the men, especially the younger ones, worshipped.
'The colonel copped it from a stray bullet. It must have been a sniper ...
just a neat little hole in the middle of his forehead, no bigger than a tickey,
    and he dropped dead in his tracks.
The major was leading us over some rough open ground between the gully
    and the far koppie
when a burst of machine gun bullets smacked from the kloof, tearing him
    open;
he was a long way ahead of us all and as he fell he shouted:
'Stop! Stay where you are! Don't come near me! Look out for those machine
    guns! There's one in the antheap and one on the ledge ...
    Bring up the mortars! The rest take cover!'
Then he rolled over on his back, blood streaming all over his body, and
    with a dabble of blood on his lips he died – Christ, what a man he was!'

The boy reached for a match box, then lighting a cigarette, he continued:
'We came on them about ten minutes later, three Ities curled up on some
        straw in a sort of dugout
– as snug as a bug in a rug – and they were sleeping . . .
The two on the outside were young, I noticed. They were all unshaven.
    The bloke in the middle had a dirty grey stubble of a beard – and that's
    all I noticed . . .'

As the boy stopped talking he moved, his hair falling in thick yellow curls
    over his forehead, his eyes.
And as I caught the soft gleam of blue behind the strands of gold
I was suddenly reminded of quiet pools of water after rain
among the golden gorse that mantle in early summer
the browning hills of Provence.

'Then I put my bayonet through each of them in turn, just in the right
    place, and they did not even grunt or murmur . . .'

There was no sadism in his voice, no savagery, no brutal pride or perverse
    eagerness to impress,
no joy, no exultation.
He spoke as if he were telling of a rugby match
in which he wasn't much interested
and in which he took no sides.

And as I looked at his eyes again
I was struck with wonderment
at their bigness, their blueness, their clarity
and how young they were, how innocent.

EL ALAMEIN John Jarmain

There are flowers now, they say, at Alamein;
Yes, flowers in the minefields now.
So those that come to view that vacant scene,
Where death remains and agony has been
Will find the lilies grow –
Flowers, and nothing that we know.

So they rang the bells for us and Alamein,
Bells which we could not hear.
And to those who heard the bells what could it mean,
That name of loss and pride, El Alamein?
– Not the murk and harm of war,
But their hope, their own warm prayer.

It will become a staid historic name,
That crazy sea of sand!
Like Troy or Agincourt its single fame
Will be the garland for our brow, our claim,
On us a fleck of glory to the end;
And there our dead will keep their holy ground.

But this is not the place that we recall,
The crowded desert crossed with foaming tracks,
The one blotched building, lacking half a wall,
The grey-faced men, sand-powered over all;
The tanks, the guns, the trucks,
The black, dark-smoking wrecks.

So be it; none but us has known that land:
El Alamein will still be only ours
And those ten days of chaos in the sand.
Others will come who cannot understand,
Will halt beside the rusty minefield wires
And find there, flowers.

ELEGY FOR AN 88 GUNNER   **Keith Douglas**

Three weeks gone and the combatants gone,
returning over the nightmare ground
we found the place again and found
the soldier sprawling in the sun.

The frowning barrel of his gun
overshadows him. As we came on
that day, he hit my tank with one
like the entry of a demon.

And smiling in the gunpit spoil
is a picture of his girl
who has written: *Steffi, Vergissmeinicht.*
in a copybook Gothic script.

We see him almost with content,
abased and seeming to have paid,
mocked by his durable equipment
that's hard and good when he's decayed.

But she would weep to see today
how on his skin the swart flies move,
the dust upon the paper eye
and the burst stomach like a cave.

For here the lover and the killer are mingled
who had one body and one heart;
and Death, who had the soldier singled
has done the lover mortal hurt.

He threw his cigarette in silence, then he said:

You can't predict in war;
It's a matter of luck, nothing less, nothing more.
Now here's an instance. Darnley copped it in the head
His third day up the blue although he'd seen the lot
In Dunkerque, Greece and Crete –
The sort that went in tidy and came out neat;
He copped it when the going wasn't even hot.
And there was little Pansy Flowers,
Machine-gunned through the guts; he bled
(and not a murmur from him) for hours
Before he jagged it in.

And you remember Bowers?
Bowers got fragmentation in the lungs and thigh;
We couldn't do a thing: the moon was high
And a hell of a bright
On that particular night.
Poor sod, he won't kip in a civvy bed.

It's queer ... I've even laughed
When blokes have chucked it in and gone daft.
I remember one that scarpered bollock–nude
One midnight, out across the dunes, calling for Mum;
You'd have thought him blewed.
He wasn't seen again – not this side of Kingdom Come.

One job that I really funked
Was when Fat Riley bunked
From a Jerry leaguer on a getaway.
We found him blind, with both hands gone.
When we'd got him back inside the lines
He'd only say
Over and over, 'the mines, the mines, the mines'.
It's the lucky ones get dead:
He's still alive. I wonder if his wife understands
How you can't even shoot yourself without your hands.

WAR IN THE EAST

Moves in the rocks with inching fingers.
We among the feathery banana trees
Imagine for him his aim: the steel helmet
And English face filling the backsight's V.
Again as it was last time, that spurting noise,
Thud, and the writhing figure in long grass.

Until we match precision with precision:
We move ten men to one and have him then.

I saw the sniper in the afternoon. The rifle
Lay there beside him neatly like his shooting,
The grass twined all about his cap.
He had killed neatly but we had set
Ten men about him to write death in jags
Cutting and spoiling on his face and broken body.

From *THE JUNGLE*   **Alun Lewis**

In mole-blue indolence the sun
Plays idly on the stagnant pool
In whose grey bed black swollen leaf
Holds Autumn rotting like an unfrocked priest.
The crocodile slides from the ochre sand
And drives the great translucent fish
Under the boughs across the running gravel.
Windfalls of brittle mast crunch as we come
To quench more than our thirst – our selves –
Beneath this bamboo bridge, this mantled pool
Where sleep exudes a sinister content
As though all strength of mind and limb must pass
And all fidelities and doubts dissolve,
The weighted world a bubble in each head,
The warm pacts of the flesh betrayed
By the nonchalance of a laugh,
The green indifference of this sleep.

CAIN IN THE THE JUNGLE   Denys L. Jones

I have killed my brother in the jungle;
Under the green liana's clammy tangle
I hid, and pressed my trigger, and he died.

Smooth as the spotted panther crept my brother,
Never a creak of his equipment's leather,
Never a leaf dislodged nor bird offended.

With his palaeozoic prototype
My mother shared her own ungainly shape
In canverns on some slow Silurian stream;

And with the cublings played my father's sons,
Shoulder to shoulder chipped their flints and bones
Or scraped a greasy ichthyosaurus hide.

And, when the floods of purple slime receded
My brother's hutments by the apes were raided,
I lay beneath my brother's legs and cried.

Yet I have fought my brother for the planets;
I have never stopped to hear the linnets,
Or watch the cocos grow against the moon.

I have only slain him in the shadows,
I have made his slant-eyed women widows
And inherited his empty meadows.

From *BURMA CASUALTY*   **Alun Lewis**

(To Captain G. T. Morris, Indian Army)

'Your leg must go. Okay?' the surgeon said
'Take it' he said. 'I hate the bloody thing.'
Yet he was terrified – not of the knives
Nor losing the green leg (he'd often wished
He'd had a gun to shoot the damned thing off)
But of the darkness that he knew would come
And bid him enter its deep gates alone.

The nurse would help him and the orderlies.
But did they know? And could a rubber tube
Suck all that darkness out of lungs and heart?
'Open and close your fist – slowly,' the doctor said.
He did so, lying still upon his back.
The whitewashed walls, the windows bright with sky
Gathered a brilliant light above his head.
Here was the light, the promise hard and pure,
His wife's sweet body and her wilful eyes.
Her timeless love stooped down to raise him up.
He felt the white walls part – the needle pricked,
'Ten seconds and you'll fade,' the doctor said.
He lay and looked into the snowwhite skies
For all ten seconds means at such a time.
Then through the warped interstices of life
The darkness swept like water through a boat
In gouts and waves of softness, claiming him . . .

He went alone: knew nothing: and returned
Retching and blind with pain, and yet Alive.

IN ENEMY HANDS

THE THREE

Mikola Auramcyk

Translated by Vera Rich

They put them behind wire in freezing winter,
Each one, already, solemnly had vowed
To break out of captivity, to win a
Way through the woods to their own folk, somehow.

Cold storm winds over the whole camp were wailing,
Corpses lay by the wall, strewn in a string ...
Strength was departing from the body daily,
The eldest one could not live out the spring.

With grief and vengeance in the heart deep hidden,
All his companions could not help but grieve ...
Like them, their friend against his death had striven,
Once more to help the foe this world to leave.

In that night, the two fled from the barracks,
Broke through the circuit-fence close to the gate,
And with them, very carefully they carried
And brought out, from beyond the wire, their mate.

In the darkness a spring wind was breathing ...
And sitting on the grass, safely arrived,
The two felt that, now that he was in freedom
Once more, the third should straightaway revive.

CRAZED MAN IN CONCENTRATION CAMP

Agnes Gergely

Translated by Edwin Morgan

All through the march, besides bag and blanket
he carried in his hands two packages of empty boxes,
and when the company halted for a couple of minutes
he laid the two packages of empty boxes neatly at each side,
being careful not to damage or break either of them,
the parcels were of
ornamental boxes
dovetailed by sizes each to each
and tied together with packing-cord,
the top box with a picture on it.
When the truck was about to start, the sergeant
shouted something in sergeant's language,
they sprang up suddenly,
and one of the boxes rolled down to the wheel,
the smallest one, the one with the picture:
'It's fallen,' he said and made to go after it,
but the truck moved off
and his companions held his hands
while his hands held the two packages of boxes
and his tears trailed down his jacket.
'It's fallen,' he said that evening in the queue
and it meant nothing to him to be shot dead.

POEMES DES HEURES DE BUCHENWALD

André Verdet

Translated by Sally Morse and Ian Murchie

Day is withdrawing like an old king
Dispossessed of his crown
By barbarian foreigners
Alone on the road to exile
He turns back at the corner of a wood
When the frontiers of the country
Are already fading beneath his footsteps
Day is withdrawing like an old king

Night is creeping in like a beggar
That love and glory previously overwhelmed
And reflected in their lights
It challenges the passerby
And begs from him a few stars
But he hurries away murmuring
That madness is a strange thing
Night is creeping in like a beggar

Morning seems like an orphan
Always in search of a smile
From a bird's game from a flower's cry
But death alone runs to tell him
That he is one of the dead who sleep fitfully
In the close nothingness of ashes
Of the dead who are still tortured
Morning seems like an orphan

INVENTORY   **Gunter Eich**

Translated by Michael Hamburger

This is my cap,
this is my greatcoat,
and here's my shaving kit
in its linen bag.

A can of meat:
my plate, my mug,
into its tin
I've scratched my name.

Scratched it with this
invaluable nail
which I keep hidden
from covetous eyes.

My bread bag holds
two woollen socks
and a couple of things
I show to no one,

like that it serves me
as a pillow at night.
Between me and the earth
I lay this cardboard.

This pencil lead
is what I love most:
by day it writes verses
I thought up in the night.

This is my notebook
and this is my groundsheet,
this is my towel,
this is my thread.

A CAMP IN THE PRUSSIAN FOREST

Randall Jarrell

I walk beside the prisoners to the road.
Load on puffed load,
Their corpses, stacked like sodden wood,
Lie barred or galled with blood

By the charred warehouse. No one comes to-day
In the old way
To knock the fillings from their teeth;
The dark, coned, common wreath

Is plaited for their grave – a kind of grief.
The living leaf
Clings to the planted profitable
Pine if it is able;

The boughs sigh, mile on green, calm, breathing mile,
From this dead file
The planners ruled for them ... One year
They sent a million here:

Here men were drunk like water, burnt like wood.
The fat of good
and evil, the breast's star of hope
were rendered into soap.

I paint the star I sawed from yellow pine –
And plant the sign
In soil that does not yet refuse
Its usual Jews

Their first asylum. But the white, dwarfed star –
This dead white star –
Hides nothing, pays for nothing; smoke
Fouls it, a yellow joke,

The needles of the wreath are chalked with ash,
A filmy trash
Litters the black woods with the death
Of men; and one last breath

Curls from the monstrous chimney . . . I laugh aloud
Again and again;
The star laughs from its rotting shroud
Of flesh. O star of men!

ORADOUR

Jean Tardieu

For Paul Eluard

Translated by Sally Morse and Ian Murchie

Oradour has no women
Oradour has no men
Oradour has no leaves
Oradour has no stones
Oradour has no church
Oradour has no children

no smoke, no laughter
no roofs, no granaries
no haystacks, no love
no wine, no songs

Oradour I'm frightened of hearing
Oradour I do not dare
approach your wounds
your blood, your ruins
I can't, I cannot
see or hear your name

Oradour I shout and scream
each time that a heart bursts
under the assassins' blows
a terror-stricken face
two wide eyes, two red eyes
two serious eyes, two large eyes
like the night, madness
the two eyes of a small child
they will not leave me;
Oradour I no longer dare
read or pronounce your name

Oradour shame of man
Oradour eternal shame
hatred and shame for ever

Oradour has no shape or form
Oradour, women or men
Oradour has no children
Oradour has no leaves
Oradour has no church
no smoke, no girls
no evenings or mornings
no tears or songs

Oradour is only a cry
and this is the worst insult
to the village that used to live
and surely the worst shame
is to be but a cry,
that a name hated by men
a name of the shame of men
which throughout our land
is heard with trembling
a mouth without a body
which screams for all time

EUX

Jean Marcenae

Translated by Sally Morse and Ian Murchie

When they fasten their coats
A cold wind blows through our halls
When they buckle on their belts
They rattle the keys of our prison
When they click their heels
Our eyes lower in shame
Nothing is pure between them and us
Except this hand which threatens them.

GERMAN P.O.W. CAMP   **Alan White**

Here where the flies are thickest,
and the jagged strands of wire
enclose with coil and palisade
is a zoo grotesque,

where trained, potential killers
are without their fangs
and pace the cage in twos and threes,
dragging boredom with each step.
On the ground, baked hard as teak,
the motley bivouacs are strewn,
ground-sheet, silken parachute,
torn canvas, dusty blanket,
anything that serves
as parasol and parapluie.

Observe the prisoners,
blond arrogance of hair,
the athlete in their stance,
and hear their marching songs,
drum-like in cadence
and as mellow maudlin
as the feel of wine,
making an outlaw flag
wave in the heart,
hysteria its nationality.
These traits in time of war,
when all virility is at high price,
almost compel an urge to fraternise.
But then an inner voice recalls –
Dachau, the death, despair and darkness.
Rotterdam, rased flat by bombs.
Paris, festering with pompous uniforms
and the malignant swastika,
and England's scars.
In a trice I have become
the gaoler once again,
confident with hate
and quick to penalize.

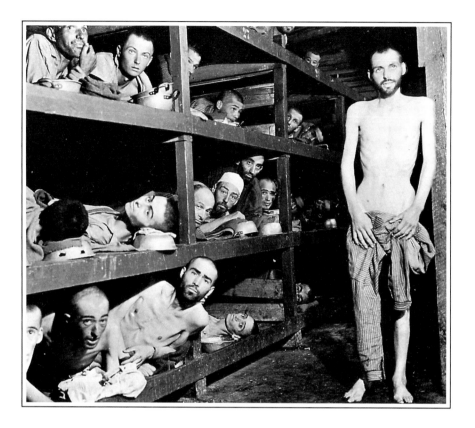

Remember the blackness of that flesh
Tarring the bones with a thin varnish
Belsen Theresenstadt Buchenwald where
Faces were a clenched despair
Knocking at the bird-song-fretted air.

Their eyes sunk jellied in their holes
Were held up to the sun like begging bowls
Their hands like rakes with finger-nails of rust
Scratched for a little kindness from the dust.
To many, in its beak, no dove brought answer.

So here am I
    Upon the German earth, beneath the German sky,
    And birds flock southward, wheeling as they fly,
    And there are morning mists, and trees turn brown,
    And the winds blow, and blow the dead leaves down,
    And lamps are earlier on, and curtains drawn,
    And nights leave frosted dew-drops on the lawn,
    And bonfire smoke goes curling up on high,
Just as on English earth, beneath an English sky.
But here am I.

BIOGRAPHIES

Phyllis Shand Allfrey
Born in 1915 in the West Indies, where her father was Crown Attorney. During the war, she worked for the London County Council as a welfare advisor to those who had been bombed. After the war, she became a founder of the Dominican Labour Party, and later was a Minister of the Federal Government.

Mikola Auramcyk
Born in 1920 into a Russian peasant family. During the war, he was taken prisoner and deported to the Ruhr as a forced labourer, working in coal mines. In 1949, he graduated from Minsk University. He has written several books.

Juliette de Bairacli-Levy
Born in Manchester. She studied biology and veterinary medicine at Manchester and Liverpool Universities, but did not qualify. Her brother and childhood sweetheart were both killed in action. During the war, she worked in the Forestry Section of the Women's Land Army. Other publications include novels and books on herbs.

John Bayliss
Born in 1919 in Gloucestershire and educated at Latymer Upper, and St Catharine's College, Cambridge. He joined the RAF and served as a flight lieutenant.

D. Van den Bogaerde
Otherwise known as the actor Dirk Bogarde. Born in 1921. He served in the Queen's Royal Regiment in Europe and the Far East. 'Steel Cathedrals' was first published in 1943.

B. G. Bonnallack
Born in 1907, and educated at Mill Hill and Clare College, Cambridge. Served with the Honourable Artillery company in Europe during the war.

David Bourne
Born in 1921 in Kent, and educated at Cranbrook. He became a pilot officer in the RAF, and was shot down and killed on 5 September 1941. Many of his poems were published by the Bodley Head in 1944.

Bertolt Brecht
Born in Augsburg in 1898. He studied medicine and worked as a medical orderly in the First World War. In 1933 he fled to Zurich and then to the USA. He returned to East Berlin in 1947, and became an Austrian citizen in 1950. He remained in East Berlin until his death in 1956.

R. P. Brett
An aircraftsman in the RAF when 'Cockerel Complex' and 'Point of View' were published in the anthology *Air Force Poetry* in 1944.

O. C. Chave
Born in 1912. Became a flight lieutenant in the RAF, and was killed in action in 1943.

Lois Clark
Trained at a college of dance and drama. When war broke out she became an ambulance driver. During the Blitz she drove a stretcher party

car in the Clapham and Brixton area of London.

Herbert Corby
Born in London in 1911. He joined the RAF and served as an armourer in a bomber squadron working on Hampden and Lancaster aircraft.

Keith Douglas
Born in 1920 and educated at Christ's Hospital and Merton College, Oxford. He was a captain in the Royal Armoured Corps, and fought at El Alamein. He took part in the Normandy landings and was killed by enemy artillery fire on 9 June 1944.

Richard Eberhart
Born in 1904 in the USA. He wrote 'The Fury of Aerial Bombardment' while a reserve officer in the US Navy. His role was to train air gunners, and he was saddened and shocked by the number who did not return from active service.

Gunter Eich
Born in 1872, and grew up in Brandenburg. He studied Law and Chinese before living as a writer in Berlin, Dresden and Paris. His first book of poems appeared in 1930. He served in the German Army, and became famous for his poems written while a prisoner of war. He died in 1972.

Olivia FitzRoy
Born in Hampshire in 1921 and educated at home by a governess. During the war she joined the Women's Royal Naval Service and became a flight direction officer. She died in 1969.

Wilfrid Gibson
Born in Northumberland in 1878. He became one of the leading Georgian poets. Poor eyesight prevented him from fighting in the First World War, but he did join the RASC. He died in 1962.

Michael Guttenbrunner
Born in 1919. He was arrested and held by the Gestapo for four months in 1938. He served in the German Army, was wounded three times and even court martialled and sentenced to death. After the war he lived in Vienna as a writer.

Bernard Gutteridge
Born in 1916 in Southampton, and educated at Cranleigh. He served with the 36th Division in Burma.

Mary Hacker
Born and brought up in London, she endured bombing raids in both the First and Second World Wars.

Norman Hampson
Born in 1922, and educated at Manchester Grammar School and University College, Oxford. He served in the Royal Navy as a sub-lieutenant on a Corvette. After the war, he became Professor of History at York University.

T. R. Hodgson
Born in 1915. He joined the RAF and was killed in action in May 1941.

Pamela Holmes
Educated at Benenden School, Sussex. Her husband, Lieutenant F. C. Hall, was posted missing believed killed in December 1942. Their daughter was born four months after his death.

Peter Huchel

Born in Berlin in 1903. He studied philosophy and literature. He served in the German Army during the war and was taken prisoner by the Russians. After the war, he was allowed to leave East Germany and settle in West Germany.

John Jarmain

An officer with the 51st Highland Division, who fought in the desert. He took part in the Normandy landings and was killed by mortar fire on 26 June 1944.

Wrenne Jarman

Worked at the Hawker aircraft works in Kingston, Surrey, during the war. She held literary gatherings at her home which were attended by poets such as Dylan Thomas. She died in 1953.

Randall Jarrell

Born in Tennessee in 1914. Having graduated from Vanderbilt University, he taught at various colleges in the USA. An author as well as a poet who published many critical essays. He died in 1965.

Denys L. Jones

Born in Britain in 1917. He went to sea before the war, then joined the army.

Sidney Keyes

Born in Kent in 1922, and educated at Tonbridge School, and Oxford. His first book of poems, *The Iron Laurel*, appeared in 1942. He was taken prisoner during the Tunisian campaign in April 1942 and died in captivity.

Uys Krige

A distinguished South African poet.

Alun Lewis

Born in 1915 at Aberdare and educated at Cowbridge Grammar School and University College, Aberystwyth. He became a schoolmaster, and then joined the Royal Engineers. He was then commissioned into the South Wales Borderers. He went to India in 1943 and was killed accidentally by his own revolver in 1944, on the Arakan front.

Jack Lindsay

Born in 1900 in Melbourne, Australia. He was educated at the University of Brisbane, then settled in England. A prolific poet and novelist, 'Squadding' was published in *New Lyrical Ballads* in 1945.

Louis MacNeice

Born in 1907 in Belfast, and educated at Marlborough and Merton College, Oxford. Before the war he lectured in Greek and Classics. At the outbreak of war he was at Cornell University in the USA, but returned to London to work for the BBC. He died in 1963.

H. B. Mallalieu

Born in 1914 in New Jersey, USA. He worked as a journalist in London before the war. He joined the Royal Artillery and saw service in the Mediterranean and Italy.

Jean Marcenae

Born in 1913 in France. He escaped from a prisoner of war camp in 1941. He wrote poetry that was very hostile to the Germans and collaborators.

Colin McIntyre

A company commander with the Black Watch.

J. G. Meddemmen

The pen name of J. G. Barker. Born in 1917, conscripted in 1940. He saw service in twelve countries.

Pimien Pancanka

Born in 1917 in Estonia. He qualified as a teacher, and then fought on a number of fronts during the war. His poetry was first published in 1933, and he has been a prolific writer since then.

Geoff Pearse

No information is available.

Edith Pickthall

Born in Britain in 1893. She trained as a maternity nurse and midwife. For most of the war she acted as an emergency midwife near Falmouth in Cornwall.

Enoch Powell

Born in 1912, and educated at King Edward VI School, Birmingham, and Trinity College, Cambridge. A Professor of Greek before the war, he joined the army and rose from the rank of private to brigadier. Awarded a military MBE in 1943. A Member of Parliament since 1950, and Minister of Health from 1960–63.

Henry Reed

Born in 1914, and educated at King Edward VI School, Birmingham, and Birmingham University. Entered the RAOC in 1941 but was released in 1942 to work in the Foreign Office.

Alan Ross

Born in 1922 and educated at Haileybury, and St John's College, Oxford. Served with the Royal Navy in the Arctic and North Seas. After the war he was with the British Council and then became editor of the *London Magazine*.

Patrick Savage

Born in 1916, and educated at Westminster School, and Christ Church, Oxford. A prisoner of war for four years. After the war, he became headmaster of Summerfields School, Oxford.

Louis Simpson

Born in 1923 in Jamaica. He went to the USA in 1940. From 1943 until the end of the war he served in the Glider Infantry of the 101st Airborne Division. He was wounded in Holland and later suffered a nervous breakdown. He has published a novel and six books of poetry.

Jean Tardieu

Born in 1903 in France. Much of his poetry was published illegally during the German occupation of France.

André Verdet

Born in 1913. He was arrested for being a member of the French Resistance in 1944 and imprisoned in Auschwitz and Buchenwald concentration camps.

James Walker

Born in 1911 in Manchester, and educated at secondary school in North Wales.

Alan White

Born in 1920. He served as a lieutenant in the Royal Artillery and was killed at Monte Cassino on 12 May 1944.

Richard Wilbur

Born in 1921 in the USA. Educated at Amherst College and Harvard University. In 1957 he was awarded the Pulitzer Prize for 'Things of This World'. He is also a translator of French literary works.

Acknowledgements

For permission to reprint copyright material the publishers gratefully acknowledge the following:

Shepheard-Walwyn (Publishers) Ltd and the Salamander Oasis Trust for 'Medjez-el-bab' by C. H. Bevan from *From Oasis into Italy*; the Peters Fraser and Dunlop Group Ltd for 'Steel Cathedrals' by D. Van den Bogaerde; Methuen London for 'I Read About Tank Battles' and 'To the German Soldiers in the East' by Bertolt Brecht, translated by John Willett, from *Poems 1913–1956;* The Executors of the Estate of Lois Clark for 'Flashback'; *'Vergissmeinnicht'* ('Elegy for an 88 Gunner') by Keith Douglas © Marie J. Douglas 1978. Reprinted from *The Complete Poems of Keith Douglas* edited by Desmond Graham (1978) by permission of Oxford University Press; Shepheard-Walwyn (Publishers) Ltd and the Salamander Oasis Trust for 'War's Benefit' and 'To a German Airman' by Brian Gallie from *Return to Oasis*; Mr Michael Gibson and Macmillan, London and Basingstoke, for 'Shells' and 'When the Plane Dived' by Wilfrid Gibson; 'Achtung! Achtung!' by Mary Hacker from *The Times Literary Supplement* 13 October 1961 © Times Newspapers Ltd 1961; Michael Hamburger for his translations of 'Marching Past' by Michael Guttenbrunner, 'Inventory' by Gunter Eich and 'Winter Billet' by Peter Huchel, from *German Poetry 1910–1975* edited by Michael Hamburger (Carcanet New Press Ltd); Shepheard-Walwyn (Publishers) Ltd and the Salamander Oasis Trust for 'The Taking of the Koppie' by Uys Krige from *Return to Oasis*, and 'Infantryman' by Colin McIntyre from *From Oasis into Italy*; Faber & Faber Ltd for an extract from 'Autumn Journal' from *The Collected Poems of Louis MacNeice*; This England Books for 'High Flight' by John Magee from *The Complete Works of John Magee* edited by Stephen Garnett; Edwin Morgan for his translation of 'Crazed Man in Concentration Camp' by Agnes Gergely; Shepheard-Walwyn (Publishers) Ltd and the Salamander Oasis Trust for 'At Sea' by Geoff Pearse from *Return to Oasis*; The Rt Hon. J. Enoch Powell, MBE for 'The Net' from *Dancer's End*; The Literary Executor of the Henry Reed Estate for 'Naming of Parts' by Henry Reed from *A Map of Verona*; Alan Ross for 'Survivors' and 'Destroyers in the Arctic' from *Blindfold Games* (Collins Harvill); Vernon Scannell for 'Walking Wounded'; Faber & Faber Ltd for 'Memento' by Stephen Spender from *Collected Poems*.

While every effort has been made to secure permission, in some cases it has proved impossible to trace the copyright holders. The Publishers apologise for this apparent negligence.

For permission to reproduce illustrations the publishers gratefully acknowledge the Imperial War Museum, who supplied all the photographs.

Edward Hudson is greatly indebted to Ian Murchie and Sally Morse for their translations of the French poems; the staff of the Photographic Department of the Imperial War Museum for their help and enthusiasm; and Mrs Anne Powell of Palladour Books for various pieces of essential information on the poets.

Index of First Lines